ALL THIS INSIDE

Published 2019. Little Brother Books, Ground Floor,
23 Southernhay East, Exeter, Devon, EX1 1QL
Printed In Poland.

books@littlebrotherbooks.co.uk | www.littlebrotherbooks.co.uk

The Little Brother Books trademark, email and website addresses,
are the sole and exclusive properties of Little Brother Books Limited.

® and © 2019 CCA and B, LLC.
All Rights Reserved.
Licensed by Rocket Licensing Ltd.

the ELF on the SHELF®

a Christmas tradition ™

This Annual belongs to

Olivia

AND FOLLOWS THE ADVENTURES OF SCOUT ELF

Sparkles
xx

Turn the page to begin your Christmas adventure...

Welcome...

Join in the fun-filled Christmas tradition of The Elf on the Shelf® with this exciting Annual bursting with Christmas cheer.

PUZZLES GALORE

Inside is packed full of festive fun! Crack the code to reveal a cheeky message, spot the differences between the elf pictures and follow the trails to see who will put the star on top of the Christmas tree.

yum!

DELICIOUS RECIPES

Christmas wouldn't be Christmas without a treat or two! Surprise your family with some homemade festive cookies and discover the elves' favourite hot chocolate recipes.

FILL-IN ACTIVITIES

Grab a pen and become the star of this Annual! Fill in a fact file all about your Scout Elf, write a letter to Santa and keep a log of your Christmas adventure with your elf.

Dear Santa,

My name is _____
and I live in _____
I hope you're as excited about Christmas as I am!
My Scout Elf is called _____
They have been watching me and my family
for you. I've enclosed a list of some of
the kind things we've been doing.
The present I would most like for Christmas is _____

On Christmas Eve, I'll leave a treat of _____
_____ for you and your reindeer.
I hope you enjoy it!

**Have fun in the North Pole,
Love from**

NORTH POLE

Santa's Mail Centre
Unit 9 Madingley Court
Chippenham Drive
Milton Keynes
Buckinghamshire
MK10 0BZ.

ELF IDEAS

Discover how to give your elf a helping hand to find unique hiding spots. All you need to do is leave some supplies to inspire them!

CHRISTMAS CRAFTS

Get crafty with some fabulous festive makes! Create your own Christmas tree decorations, make an awesome elf Christmas card and cut out some fun selfie props.

FIND ME!

Scout Elves are experts at hiding. Can you find this little elf hiding on every double page in this Annual?

Meet the
SCOUT ELVES

Santa has a special group of trusted helpers around the world who help make Christmas happen. Let's find out more about these magical Scout Elves.

AN IMPORTANT JOB

Scout Elves have a very important Christmas job – they help Santa manage his nice list. After being adopted by a family, a Scout Elf finds a spot in their home to sit and watch over their Christmas adventures during the day. Then, once everyone in the house is fast asleep, the elf flies home to the North Pole to report back to Santa. In the morning, before anyone is awake, the Scout Elf returns to its family and waits in a new spot for someone to find them.

SCOUT ELF MAGIC

A Scout Elf's heart is full of Christmas magic and when they are named by their family, the magic is activated. This gives Scout Elves the power to fly to and from the North Pole at lightning speed.

SPECIAL TRAINING

Before Scout Elves depart from the North Pole, they are trained to run, jump and climb by the elite Scout Elf Training Team. They also learn how to create fun and exciting hiding spots in homes around the world. Elves need to stay up-to-date with the latest scouting tips and tricks.

NORTH POLE FUN

Each night, before Scout Elves head back to their families, there's always time for a little North Pole fun! Some elves play their favourite sport, others like to go for a stroll in the snow and some can't resist cosying up around a flickering campfire.

A HELPING HAND

As well as helping Santa update his nice list, Scout Elves do all kinds of other jobs for Santa. They sort the post, help in the reindeer stables and complete special duties in the North Pole.

DID YOU KNOW?
Scout Elves are the only elves who interact with humans.

NAME GENERATOR

Being given a name is very important to Scout Elves as this is when they get their magic. Use the name generator below to work out what your elf name is.

How it works

Take the initial of your first name and the month you were born, then check what they stand for in the lists below. For example, if your name is Jack and you were born in May, your Scout Elf name is Frosty McJingles.

A = Cinnamon
B = Marshmallow
C = Jingle
D = Holly
E = Peppy
F = Shiny
G = Christmas
H = Ace
I = Buddy

J = Frosty
K = Jolly
L = Snowy
M = Bauble
N = Snowball
O = Cocoa
P = Sparkle
Q = Tinsel
R = Snowflake

S = Magic
T = Festive
U = Star
V = Lucky
W = Jazzy
X = Gingerbread
Y = Icicle
Z = Peppermint

January = Brightstar
February = Frostwell
March = Gingerberg
April = Red Hat
May = McJingles
June = Twinkle Toes

July = Sugar Plum
August = Snowman
September = Frostington
October = O'Mittens
November = Candy Cane
December = Northstar

The Name Generator

First name

Surname

Scout Elf name

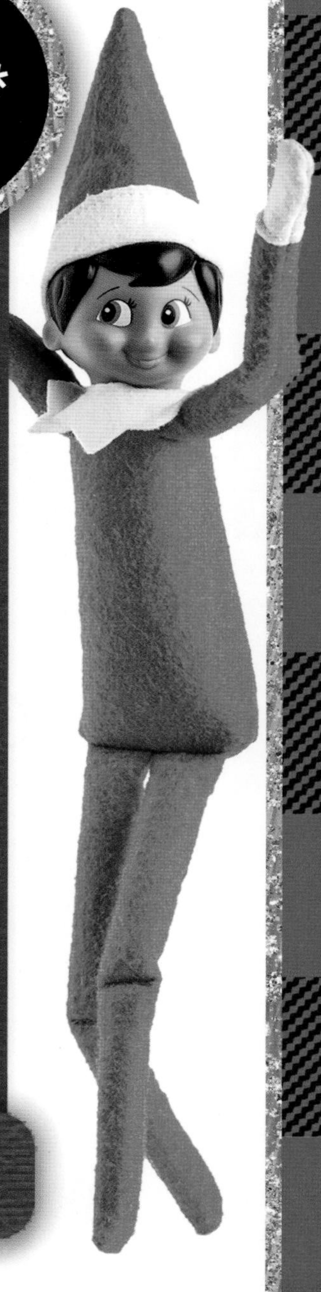

NAME

My Scout ELF

Each of Santa's trusted helpers is one of a kind. Fill in this fact file all about your own special elf.

My Scout Elf's name is

I chose that name because

I ADOPTED THEM ON

But they don't like eating

Their favourite song is

Their favourite place to hide is

These are the things I've put in my elf's keepsake box

Here's a picture of my elf.

DRAW YOUR
ELF OR STICK
A PHOTO OF
THEM HERE.

My Elf's Personality

Tick the words that best describe your elf.

- ☐ CHEEKY
- ☐ BRAVE
- ☐ KIND
- ☐ ADVENTUROUS
- ☐ THOUGHTFUL
- ☐ FUNNY

Christmas is Coming

These Christmassy ideas will make sure your whole family is in the festive spirit by the time your Scout Elf returns, or you adopt a new North Pole helper.

SEASON'S GREETINGS

Let family and friends know you're thinking of them by making and sending Christmas cards. Use the two fun templates on **pages 32-34** or design your own.

Twinkling lights

Take a family walk or drive around your local area to see the Christmas lights. Is there a particular street that is always lit up or shops that have magical window displays?

Festive Film

Grab some popcorn and snuggle up on the sofa to watch your family's favourite Christmas movie.

Warming Drink

DECK THE HALLS

Have fun decorating your house and tree. Don't forget to blast out Christmas tunes while you work!

Warm up from the cold with a mug of delicious hot chocolate.
See **pages 46 and 47** for the elves' favourite cocoa recipes.

15

A Warm Welcome

Welcoming home your Scout Elf or saying hello to a new elf is so exciting! These easy ideas will make their arrival even more special.

Bright Lights

Create a runway of lights leading to your front door so your elf will know exactly where to land.

ELF MESSAGE

WELCOME

Make a banner with a special message for your elf. Hang it somewhere where they'll be sure to see it when they arrive.

GIVE A GIFT

Leave a thoughtful gift for your elf to open on their arrival. Elves love anything that's been handmade with love!

Mini Treats

All elves have a sweet tooth so bake a delicious treat for them to enjoy. Better still, make it elf sized!

Helping Hand

Leave some supplies out so that your elf can create their own clever arrival surprise. Here are three ideas for when they come flying through your door.

1

Leave a whiteboard marker pen so your elf can write a message on a mirror for you.

2

Place a gift box full of shredded paper in an easy-to-spot location. All your elf will have to do is snuggle inside and wait for you to find them.

3

Leave a jar of peppermints for your elf to pop out of. Stick a piece of paper on the jar and leave a pen nearby so your elf can write you a message.

PERSONALITY QUIZ

Just like humans, every Scout Elf is one-of-a-kind. Discover more about your elf's personality by answering the fun questions below.

1
In the morning, my Scout Elf can be found:

A. Playing a funny joke

B. Dangling from a high shelf

C. Making something

2
I can always count on my elf to:

A. Make me laugh

B. Amaze me every day

C. Make something inventive

3
One of my elf's favourite hobbies might be:

A. Telling funny jokes

B. Flying through the night sky

C. Writing a fun riddle

4
I think my elf would love to go:

A. To an amusement park

B. On a backpacking adventure

C. To an art gallery

5

My elf's favourite outfit might be:

A. A funny fancy dress

B. A sports kit

C. Anything sparkly

6

In the North Pole, my elf is most likely to:

A. Have a snowball fight

B. Go on a fast sleigh ride

C. Make lots of presents

MOSTLY A - PLAYFUL!

Your cheeky elf likes to plan silly surprises that will make the family smile. They love finding funny hiding spots, playing jokes and making you laugh.

MOSTLY B - ADVENTUROUS!

Daring feats are no problem for your brave elf! They adore adventure and can often be found scaling dizzy heights or dangling from high places.

MOSTLY C - CREATIVE!

Making imaginative hiding spots with everyday objects is what your creative elf does best! They love coming up with new ways to surprise and delight you.

FUNNY MESSAGE

Santa's Scout Elves have written a cheeky joke for him. Can you crack the code to reveal what it says?

Answers on pages 76-77

YOUR TURN!

Use this space to write your own joke for Santa. Cut it out and leave it next to your Scout Elf so they can deliver it to the North Pole.

Make sure you read page 22 before you cut out your joke.

WARNING! ADULT GUIDANCE IS NEEDED FOR THIS ACTIVITY.

SPOT THE SCOUT ELVES

Using their special hiding ability, 10 elves have hidden in the room below. Can you spot them all?

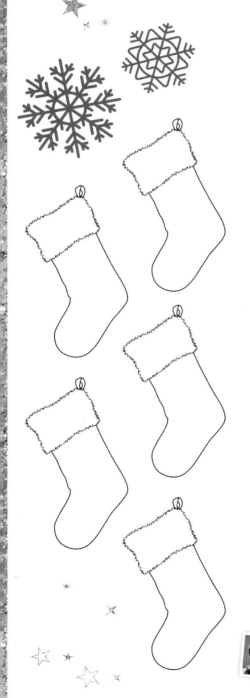

COLOUR A STOCKING AS YOU SPOT EACH ELF.

Answers on pages 76-77

Thoughtful Friends

These Scout Elves are making a mug of hot chocolate for Santa. Use your favourite pens to colour this cosy scene.

Sugar

Coco

Letter to Santa

Deep in the North Pole, covered in snow, sits Santa's mail room grotto where he reads every single letter he receives. Use the template opposite to write your own letter to Santa.

How to Send your letter

When you've filled in your letter to Santa, written your list of kind deeds and drawn your picture, carefully cut everything out, put it in an envelope and post it to the address on the right. This is one of Santa's certified UK mail centres and is filled with humans who work for Santa. They will pass your letter on to the man himself!

Santa's Mail Centre
Unit 9 Madingley Court
Chippenham Drive
Milton Keynes
Buckinghamshire
MK10 0BZ

WARNING!
ADULT GUIDANCE IS NEEDED FOR THIS ACTIVITY.

DID YOU KNOW?
60% of children's letters to Santa include a colourful drawing.

NORTH POLE

Dear Santa,

My name is _____.

and I live in _____.

I hope you're as excited about Christmas as I am!

My Scout Elf is called _____.

They have been watching me and my family
for you. I've enclosed a list of some of
the kind things we've been doing.

The present I would most like for Christmas is

_____.

On Christmas Eve, I'll leave a treat of _____
_____ for you and your reindeer.

I hope you enjoy it!

Have fun in the North Pole, Love from

_____

Santa
X

Write a list of some of the kind things you and your family have been doing.

My Kind Deeds

_____
_____
_____
_____
_____
_____
_____

Draw a picture for Santa in this space.

Make sure you've read **page 28** before you cut out each piece.

ACTS OF *Kindness*

The Scout Elves are always on the lookout for kind deeds to report back to Santa. Here are some ideas to help you spread kindness all year round.

Share your toys with your brother or sister.

Say 'thank you' when your parents do something for you.

Give some toys to a charity shop.

Make a card to cheer someone up.

Tell your best friend why they're so great.

Write a nice note to a friend.

Comfort a friend if they hurt themselves.

Donate something to a food bank.

Tidy your bedroom without being asked.

Ask someone to play with you if they're on their own.

DID YOU KNOW?

Santa's Elf Pets® Saint Bernard pups gather Christmas spirit which is created when children do something kind. They store it in the barrel around their neck and on Christmas Eve it's made into Christmas magic so Santa can fly around the world.

SWEET TREATS

Scout Elves love nothing more than a festive sweet treat. Can you find the yummy words below hidden in the wordsearch?

CANDY	CHOCOLATE	PUDDING
COOKIES	GINGERBREAD	BISCUITS
SWEETS	CAKES	ICING

Here I am

O	U	K	K	D	Y	K	B	U	B	G
S	T	E	E	W	S	X	S	C	I	R
C	V	C	Q	W	S	E	H	N	S	B
A	E	U	E	Q	I	O	G	U	C	N
K	T	E	S	K	C	E	P	W	U	F
E	T	X	O	O	R	S	U	K	I	Y
S	F	O	L	B	P	H	D	B	T	D
K	C	A	R	L	X	K	D	U	S	N
V	T	E	G	N	I	C	I	V	L	A
E	A	P	Q	S	X	K	N	H	E	C
D	G	M	M	V	D	E	G	I	X	Z

Answers on pages 76-77

Cookie Creations

This recipe makes about 12 shortbread biscuits.

Make Christmas cookies Mrs. Claus would be proud of with these fun, festive ideas. Don't forget to leave one for your Scout Elf.

YOU WILL NEED

- 170g plain flour
- 55g caster sugar
- 115g softened butter
- Cookie cutters

How to Make

1. Preheat the oven to 160°C (320°F/Gas mark 3).

2. Put the flour and sugar in a bowl and rub in the butter – the butter has to be super soft so leave it out of the fridge for a few hours before baking.

3. Knead the ingredients until they form a dough and then put the dough in the fridge for a half an hour to make it firm.

4. Roll the dough out so it's about 1/2 cm thick and cut it into shapes.

5. Bake your biscuits for 15 minutes until they start to turn golden brown.

6. Let them cool and then decorate using one of the ideas on the next page.

Crunchy Candy Canes

Drizzle melted white chocolate onto candy cane shaped biscuits. Crush up a real candy cane and sprinkle it onto the melted chocolate to add a minty crunch.

Reindeer Cookies

Pipe chocolate icing antlers and eyes onto round biscuits to make these cute reindeer cookies. Don't forget to add a chocolate drop nose.

Tasty Trees

Half dip tree shaped biscuits into melted chocolate and add colourful sprinkles. Wait for the chocolate to harden and enjoy your tasty treats.

Christmas Light Delight

Cover a round biscuit with glacé icing (made by mixing drops of water with sifted icing sugar) and leave it to harden. Carefully pipe a U shape with chocolate icing then stick coloured chocolate beans on for Christmas lights.

WARNING!
ADULT GUIDANCE IS NEEDED FOR THIS ACTIVITY.

CHRISTMAS GREETINGS

Scout Elves love getting crafty at Christmas! Join in the fun by decorating these cards to send to friends or family.

YOU WILL NEED

- Scissors
- Coloured pens or pencils
- Glue
- Glitter

Why not make a card for Santa and leave it with your Scout Elf? If it's disappeared by the morning, you'll know they've delivered it to him in the North Pole!

How to Make

1. Ask an adult to help you cut out both cards.

2. Choose your favourite pens or pencils and colour in the picture on the top card.

3. Decorate your cards with glitter to add a bit of festive sparkle.

4. Fold both cards in half along the line in the middle.

5. Write your cards and deliver them to your friends or family.

WARNING! ADULT GUIDANCE IS NEEDED FOR THIS ACTIVITY.

HAVE A

Magical

Christmas!

Have your Elf a

Merry

Christmas

Hope your day is full of festive fun!

Spread some Christmas cheer!

FESTIVE FUNNIES!

Fun-loving Scout Elves like to make others laugh. Here are some of their favourite jokes to try out on your friends and family.

What do elves learn at school?

The elf-abet!

Why is it so cold at Christmas?

Because it's Decembrrrrr!

How do snowmen get around?

They ride an icicle!

What falls but never hurts itself?

Snow!

Why are Christmas trees bad at sewing?

They always drop their needles!

What comes at the end of Christmas day?

The letter Y!

FESTIVE FAVES

Christmas is coming! Look carefully at the close-ups below and see if you can work out these Scout Elves' favourite festive things.

1

2

CHECK THE PHOTOS FOR CLUES!

3

4

5

Answers on pages 76-77

SUPER EASY DECS

Make your house look as festive as Santa's grotto with these easy-to-make Christmas decorations! They're super quick to do too.

CUPCAKE TREE

YOU WILL NEED

- Different coloured cupcake cases
- Glue
- Sticky stars
- Scissors
- Thin ribbon

REINDEER DECORATION

YOU WILL NEED

- Small, clean twigs
- Glue
- Googly eyes
- Large buttons
- Thin ribbon

How to Make

1. Fold four cupcake cases in half and then fold one of them in half again.

2. Glue the cases together to make a Christmas tree shape with the smaller one at the top.

3. Decorate your tree with sticky stars.

4. Glue a loop of thin ribbon to the top of the tree so you can hang your decoration.

How to Make

1. Glue two twigs together to make a V shape.

2. Glue a third twig halfway up the V shape.

3. Glue on googly eyes and a button for a nose.

4. Tie a piece of thin ribbon in the middle of the third twig so you can hang your decoration up.

LOLLY STICK STAR

YOU WILL NEED

- Coloured craft lolly sticks
- Glitter glue
- Glue
- Scissors
- Thin ribbon

BUTTON BAUBLES

YOU WILL NEED

- Green felt
- Scissors
- Different coloured buttons
- Glue
- Thin ribbon

How to Make

1. Decorate your lolly sticks with glitter glue and leave to dry.

2. Take five lolly sticks and arrange them in a star shape then glue them together.

3. When the glue is dry, glue a loop of thin ribbon to one of the star's points so you can hang it up.

How to Make

1. Cut a Christmas tree shape from green felt.

2. Glue buttons onto your tree as baubles.

3. Snip a small hole in the top of the tree and thread a piece of thin ribbon through.

4. Tie the ribbon to make a loop so your decoration can hang.

WARNING!
ADULT GUIDANCE IS NEEDED FOR THIS ACTIVITY.

My December Journey

Use this log to record your adventures with your Scout Elf each day in the countdown to Christmas.

1st

Where my Scout Elf was hiding:

What I did today:

What my elf will report back to Santa:

Today I have been:

2nd

Where my Scout Elf was hiding:

What I did today:

What my elf will report back to Santa:

Today I have been:

3rd

Where my Scout Elf was hiding:

What I did today:

What my elf will report back to Santa:

Today I have been:

4th

Where my Scout Elf was hiding:

What I did today:

What my elf will report back to Santa:

Today I have been:

5th

Where my Scout Elf was hiding:

What I did today:

What my elf will report back to Santa:

Today I have been:

6th

Where my Scout Elf was hiding:

What I did today:

What my elf will report back to Santa:

Today I have been:

7th

Where my Scout Elf was hiding:

What I did today:

What my elf will report back to Santa:

Today I have been:

8th

Where my Scout Elf was hiding:

What I did today:

What my elf will report back to Santa:

Today I have been:

9th

Where my Scout Elf was hiding:

What I did today:

What my elf will report back to Santa:

Today I have been:

10th

Where my Scout Elf was hiding:

What I did today:

What my elf will report back to Santa:

Today I have been:

11th

Where my Scout Elf was hiding:

What I did today:

What my elf will report back to Santa:

Today I have been:

12th

Where my Scout Elf was hiding:

What I did today:

What my elf will report back to Santa:

Today I have been:

13th

Where my Scout Elf was hiding:

What I did today:

What my elf will report back to Santa:

Today I have been:

14th

Where my Scout Elf was hiding:

What I did today:

What my elf will report back to Santa:

Today I have been:

15th

Where my Scout Elf was hiding:

What I did today:

What my elf will report back to Santa:

Today I have been:

16th

Where my Scout Elf was hiding:

What I did today:

What my elf will report back to Santa:

Today I have been:

17th

Where my Scout Elf was hiding:

What I did today:

What my elf will report back to Santa:

Today I have been:

18th

Where my Scout Elf was hiding:

What I did today:

What my elf will report back to Santa:

Today I have been:

19th

Where my Scout Elf was hiding:

What I did today:

What my elf will report back to Santa:

Today I have been:

20th

Where my Scout Elf was hiding:

What I did today:

What my elf will report back to Santa:

Today I have been:

21st

Where my Scout Elf was hiding:

What I did today:

What my elf will report back to Santa:

Today I have been:

22nd

Where my Scout Elf was hiding:

What I did today:

What my elf will report back to Santa:

Today I have been:

23rd

Where my Scout Elf was hiding:

What I did today:

What my elf will report back to Santa:

Today I have been:

24th

Where my Scout Elf was hiding:

What I did today:

What my elf will report back to Santa:

Today I have been:

Cocoa Delights

Scout Elves are experts in all things sweet – especially hot chocolate. Here are some of their favourite recipes for you to try.

WARNING!
ADULT GUIDANCE IS NEEDED FOR THIS ACTIVITY.

Candy Cane Cocoa

Why not combine two of the elves' favourite sweet treats – candy canes and hot chocolate? Simply crush up a mint candy cane and let it simmer as you heat up your cocoa, then add another cane as a stirrer. Don't forget to top with whipped cream and sprinkles!

Cookies and Cream

Cover your hot chocolate with a big swirl of whipped cream then crush one of your favourite biscuits to sprinkle on the top. Make sure you have a few extra cookies for dunking! Mmmmmmm!

Hot and Cold

For the coolest hot chocolate, add an edible snowman! Join three marshmallows together with a cocktail stick, use pretzel sticks for arms and legs and draw on a face and buttons with icing. Don't forget to add an orange sweet for a carrot nose.

Cinnamon Surprise

Give your hot chocolate a burst of festive flavour by adding ¼ teaspoon of cinnamon. To finish it off, add squirty cream and sprinkle a little more cinnamon on top.

Melted Marshmallows

While your cocoa is still piping hot, sprinkle a few miniature marshmallows on top. The marshmallows will begin to melt into the hot chocolate to create a cup of squidgy, chocolatey, marshmallow yumminess!

NORTH POLE FACTS

Your Scout Elf has gathered some fascinating facts just for you. Read on to learn more about the exciting things that happen in their snowy North Pole home.

Santa's Elf Pets® Reindeer wear a magic heart charm around their necks to store the Christmas spirit needed to make Santa's sleigh fly on Christmas Eve.

SANTA RECEIVES MORE THAN 5 MILLION LETTERS EACH CHRISTMAS.

For a human, seeing a Scout Elf move is as rare as seeing Santa on Christmas Eve.

Scout Elves know more than 6,000 languages.

the ELF on the SHELF® a Christmas tradition™

ELVES ZIP AROUND SANTA'S MAIL ROOM SORTING THE POST AT **94MPH.**

AN AVERAGE OF 57 TONS OF POST ARRIVES AT THE NORTH POLE EVERY DAY.

Santa's Elf Pets® Saint Bernard pups collect Christmas cheer in the barrels around their necks – this is released on Christmas Eve to keep the North Pole magical.

Santa's favourite joke is:

What do you call an elf who sings?

A wrapper!

24,727,543 is the greatest number of letters Santa has received on one day.

Christmas Candy

This Scout Elf has been dreaming of Mrs Claus's festive candy all the way back to the North Pole. Can you help her through the maze grid to reach the sweets?

Follow the Christmas pictures in this order to get from start to finish.

1 2 3

START →				

				FINISH ↓

Answers on pages 76-77

HIDING OUT

Scout Elves use their active imagination to come up with clever hiding spots. Join the dots to reveal where this elf has chosen to hide.

51

PARTY PLANNING

What better way to celebrate the festive season than with a party for friends, family and, of course, your Scout Elf! Here's how to plan the perfect Christmas bash.

Send your invites

Make a list of who you want to invite, then make and send your party invitations. See the page opposite for a template you can photocopy. Don't forget to sprinkle on some glitter to add a bit of sparkle!

Deck the House!

Your house is probably already looking pretty Christmassy, but you can always add more decorations! Fairy lights will help bring a little bit of Christmas magic to your event.

Plan your Menu

Decide what food you'd like to serve at your party and make it in advance. Include a mixture of sweet and savoury treats that fit the festive theme of your celebration. See **pages 54-55** for some fun party snacks ideas.

CHOOSE THE ENTERTAINMENT

Make a playlist of Christmas classics and choose some fun party games to play – see **pages 56-57** for ideas. You could also bring out your selfie props from **pages 64-65** for some great photo opportunities!

Please come to our

Christmas party

On _____

In the _____ room

It'll be lots of fun!

Leave this invite for your Scout Elf so they don't miss any of the fun!

Please come to our

Christmas party

On _____

In the _____ room

It'll be lots of fun!

Make sure you read page 54 before you cut out your invites.

FESTIVE PARTY

PARTY FOOD

Amaze your guests with these fun party snacks.
They're easy to make but look really impressive.

MINI PIZZAS

YOU WILL NEED

- Packet of pizza dough mix
- Tomato puree
- Cheese (grated)
- Rolling pin
- Star shaped cookie cutter

How to Make

1. Make up the pizza dough according to the instructions on the packet.
2. Roll out the dough and cut out star shapes to make your pizza bases.
3. Part bake the bases according to the instructions on the packet.
4. Spread a thin layer of tomato puree on your bases then top with a little grated cheese. Bake in the oven according to the instructions on the packet.
5. Leave your star shaped pizzas to cool then serve them cold at your party – mmmmm, delicious!

CHRISTMAS PUD BISCUITS

YOU WILL NEED

- Packet of chocolate digestive biscuits
- Icing sugar
- Red chocolate beans
- Green jelly diamonds

How to Make

1. Make a thick glacé icing by adding drops of water to sifted icing sugar and stirring well.
2. Drizzle the icing over half of the chocolate side of a biscuit.
3. Stick on a red chocolate bean for a holly berry and two green jelly diamonds for holly leaves.
4. Leave the icing to harden then store your Christmas pudding biscuits in an airtight container until your party.

BANANA SNOWMEN

YOU WILL NEED

- Bananas
- Strawberries
- Green grapes
- Raisins
- Carrots
- Kebab sticks

How to Make

1. Slice a banana and carefully push three slices onto a kebab stick to make the snowman's body and head.
2. Cut a strawberry in half and add that to the kebab stick to make a hat.
3. Push a green grape onto the kebab stick to make a bobble for your snowman's strawberry hat.
4. Gently push raisins into the banana circles to make the snowman's eyes and buttons.
5. Cut a small triangle shape from a peeled carrot and push it into the banana face to make the snowman's carrot nose.
6. Serve your fruity snowmen kebabs as soon as you've made them.

If you want to serve cookies and hot chocolate at your party, see pages 30-31 and 46-47 for recipe ideas.

CAKE TOPPERS

YOU WILL NEED

- Glue
- Thin card
- Scissors
- Sticky tape
- Cocktail sticks

How to Make

1. Cut this page out and glue it onto thin card.
2. Carefully cut out the cake toppers.
3. Use sticky tape to attach a cocktail stick to the back of each cake topper.
4. Use the cake toppers to decorate a big cake for everyone to share at your festive party.

WARNING!
ADULT GUIDANCE IS NEEDED FOR THIS ACTIVITY.

Make sure you read page 56 before you cut out your cake toppers.

GAMES GALORE

SCAVENGER HUNT

Finding things is so much fun! Divide your party guests into teams and give them each a copy of the list below, or make up your own. The first team to find all of the things on the list is the winner.

- [ ] SOMETHING SHINY
- [ ] A KEY
- [ ] SOMETHING YOU COULD FIT IN A MATCHBOX
- [ ] DICE
- [ ] A CHRISTMAS CARD
- [ ] SOMETHING OLDER THAN YOU ARE
- [ ] A COIN
- [ ] A RED PEN OR CRAYON
- [ ] SOMETHING HOMEMADE
- [ ] A CHRISTMAS DECORATION
- [ ] A GLOVE
- [ ] A BOOK WITH AN ANIMAL ON THE COVER

Fun-loving Scout Elves adore party games! Why not liven up your party with a few of their favourites?

Pin the Tail on the Reindeer

This classic party game has been given a Christmas twist! Here's how to play:

Cut out the reindeer picture and tails on the opposite page.

Attach a small piece of adhesive putty to the top of each tail.

Stick the reindeer picture on a wall.

Give a tail to the first player, blindfold them and spin them around three times. The player must then stick their tail onto the reindeer picture.

Take it in turns to have a go. The player who sticks their tail the closest to where it should be is the winner.

Make sure you read page 58 before you cut out your game.

WARNING!
ADULT GUIDANCE IS NEEDED FOR THIS ACTIVITY.

the ELF on the SHELF®
a Christmas tradition

57

Christmas Round-up

Fill in these pages as a record of what you and your Scout Elf have been up to this Christmas. And remember, it's never too early to start planning next year's festive fun!

Good Deeds

This year, I have been mostly ✔

☐ NAUGHTY
☐ NICE

This is what I think my elf will have reported back to Santa

The kindest thing I did was

TOP HIDEOUTS

My favourite elf hiding place was

The hardest place to find my elf was

My elf made me laugh by

SWAPPING GIFTS

Some of the presents I left for my elf were

_____

_____

My elf left these things for me

_____

_____

STICK A SELFIE OF YOU AND YOUR ELF HERE.

Write your names and the date here!

Looking Forwards

Here are some ideas for my elf's arrival next Christmas

_____

_____

I think these would be good places for them to hide

_____

_____

SPOTTED!

Can you find the Scout Elf that looks **exactly** the same as this one in the elf jumble below?

Answers on pages 76-77

Christmas Cheer

Say 'freeze'! This Scout Elf is smiling for a photo in the North Pole with some of Santa's Elf Pets®. Can you spot **five** differences between the two pictures?

Colour a bauble each time you spot a difference.

Answers on pages 76-77

SCOUT ELF IDEAS

Elves are trained to find the best places to perch and watch their families. You can help them create a great hiding spot by leaving some simple supplies.

EYE EYE!

Cheeky elves love having fun with googly eyes! Leave some out for your elf and see what ideas they come up with.

A Comfy Spot

This elf looks happy hiding amongst the soft toys. Why not put all your teddies in one place and see what your elf does?

AIMING HIGH

Did you know that elves are great climbers? Leave some helpful supplies like these gift rosettes or a ball of string to find out what your elf can do.

ON A ROLL!

Who knew toilet rolls could be so much fun! See what hijinks your elves get up to when you leave one out for them.

Flying Fun

A simple piece of paper is a great prop to leave for your elf. Will they make a paper aeroplane like these elves have done?

SELFIES WITH YOUR ELF-IE!

Worried you'll miss your Scout Elf when they return to the North Pole? Then make an awesome elf selfie picture collage that you can look at all year round.

WARNING!
ADULT GUIDANCE IS NEEDED FOR THIS ACTIVITY.

YOU WILL NEED

- Scissors
- Craft lolly sticks
- Sticky tape
- Lots of selfie photos of you and your elf
- A large piece of thick paper or cardboard
- Glue
- Used Christmas cards

How to Make

1. Ask an adult to help you cut out the selfie props on the opposite page.

2. Attach a lolly stick to each selfie prop using sticky tape.

3. Throughout December, take lots of selfies of you and your elf in their hiding places. Use the selfie props for added fun!

4. Print your photos and then arrange them on a large piece of paper or cardboard. Collages look best when the photos are various sizes, overlapping and placed at different angles, so snip away and get creative!

5. Cut out images from used Christmas cards and stick them onto your collage.

6. When you're happy with your elf selfie masterpiece, prop it up somewhere or ask an adult to help you hang it on a wall.

Why not make and decorate a cardboard frame for your picture collage?

Nice

Make sure you read page 66 before you cut out your selfie props.

FOOLING AROUND!

The cheeky Scout Elves have played a trick on Santa by mixing up the letters on these gift tags! Can you put the letters back in the right order so Santa knows what's inside each present?

1 BOKO
_ _ _ _

2 BLAL
_ _ _ _

3 GMAE
_ _ _ _

4 TYO
_ _ _

Answers on pages 76-77

SCOUT ELVES AT PLAY

These elves are having a great time chilling out in the North Pole. Fill in the blank spaces to discover what they are doing.

1

c_lou_ing a picture.

2

Reading a m__az_ne.

3

Listening to mu__c.

4

Taking a s_lf__.

Answers on pages 76-77

Festive Fashion

Santa's Scout Elves look super smart in their official red jumpsuits, but they love wearing other outfits too. Design some new clothes for these fashionable elves.

Try some ideas out here first...

DID YOU KNOW?
Mrs Claus makes all of the elves' outfits in her North Pole design studio

Try some ideas out here first…

Accessorise!

Now design some awesome accessories for the elves. Hats, earmuffs, scarfs and bags are all the rage in the North Pole!

TRUE OR FALSE?

Santa has sent you a special assignment. Test your Scout Elf knowledge by answering true or false to the questions below.

1 Scout Elves can fly.

☐ TRUE ☐ FALSE

DECEMBER

2 An elf receives their magic on Christmas Eve.

☐ TRUE
☐ FALSE

3 Elves don't like sweet food.

☐ TRUE
☐ FALSE

4 Elves help Santa manage his nice list.

☐ TRUE ☐ FALSE

5 Elves live in the North Pole.

☐ TRUE ☐ FALSE

Check your answers then give yourself a score out of five.

___/5

Answers on pages 76-77

70

RACE TO THE STAR

These Scout Elves are decorating the Christmas tree, but which one will place the star on top? Follow the trails to find out.

Answers on pages 76-77

FLYING HOME

This Scout Elf has had a busy day watching his family's Christmas adventures. Can you guide him home to the North Pole to report back to Santa?

START

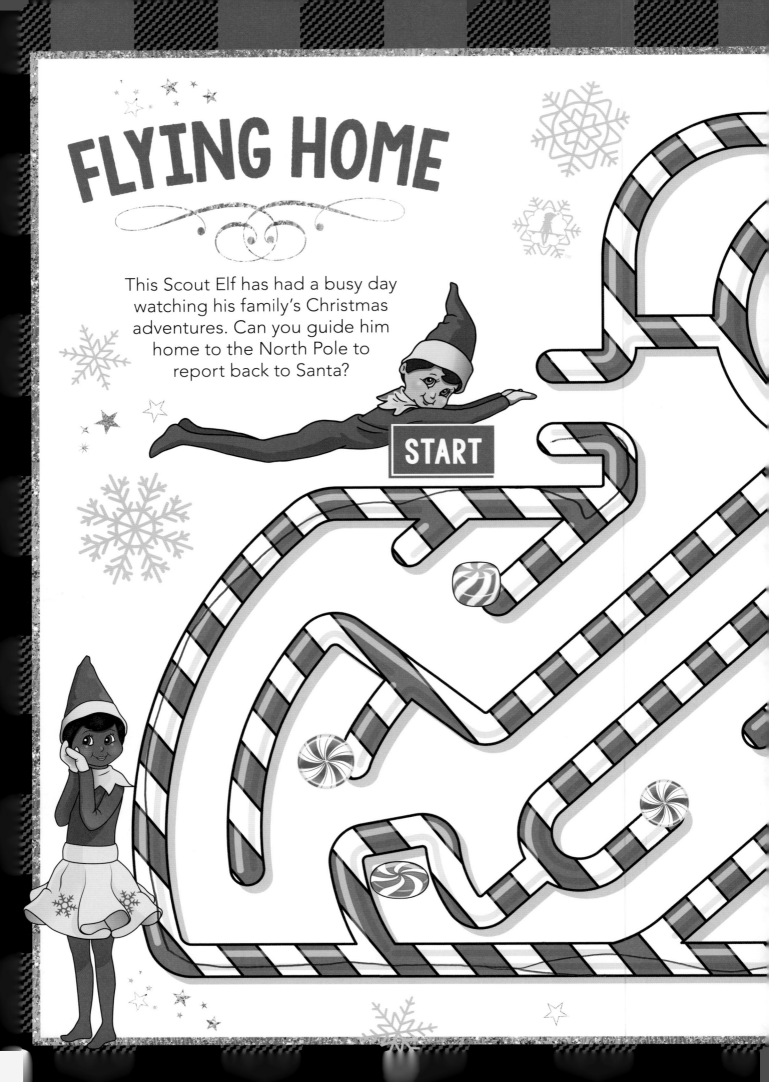

Ho-Ho-Ho

How many sweets did you pass along the way?

NORTH POLE

FINISH

Answers on pages 76-77

Time to Say Goodbye

On Christmas Eve,
Scout Elves return to the
North Pole for a very important
mission - to help Santa!
Here are some ways to say
goodbye until next year.

WRITE A NOTE

Write a goodbye letter
to your elf telling them how much
fun you've had with them this
festive season. You never know,
your elf might leave one for you to
find on Christmas morning.

GET ACTIVE

Plan one last activity for Christmas
Eve and invite your elf to watch.
Choose something the whole family
can join in with like baking cookies,
reading a festive story or watching
a Christmas classic.

Say Cheese!

Take a family selfie with your elf in their last hiding place. You could print it out and stick it up somewhere to remember your elf all year long.

CHECK FOR TRACKS

If you're lucky enough to have a white Christmas, check outside to see if your elf left any footprints in the snow before they took off. Elves have even been known to leave a snow angel as a Christmas Day surprise!

DID YOU KNOW?

Scout Elves start preparing for next year's Christmas on December 26th.

ANSWERS

Pages 20-21
Funny Message

What is red and white, red and white, red and white?

Santa rolling off a rooftop!

Pages 22-23
Spot the Scout Elves

Page 29
Sweet Treats

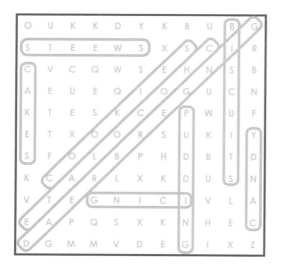

Pages 36-37
Festive Faves

1. Presents.
2. Cookies.
3. Decorations.
4. Donuts.
5. Elf Pets.

Page 50
Christmas Candy

Page 60
Spotted!

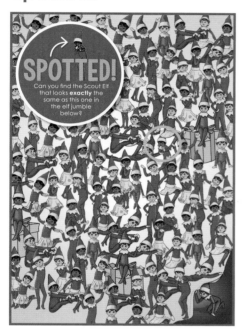

Page 61
Christmas Cheer

Page 66
Fooling Around!

1. Book.
2. Ball.
3. Game.
4. Toy.

Page 67
Scout Elves at Play

1. Colouring a picture.
2. Reading a magazine.
3. Listening to music.
4. Taking a selfie.

Page 70
True or False

1. True.

2. False – a Scout Elf receives its magic when named.

3. False – elves love sweet food.

4. True.
5. True.

Page 71
Race to the Star

Elf 2.

Pages 72-73
Flying Home